_____ **'s Lesson Assig**

(My Name)

Contents

My Name is:

My Teacher's Name is:

_____

_____

My Address is:

My Teacher's Address is:

_____

_____

_____

_____

My E-mail Address is:

My Teacher's E-mail Address is:

_____

_____

My Phone Number is:

My Teacher's Phone Number is:

_____

_____

Assignment
For Next Lesson

Date _____
Day _____
Time _____

Today's Lesson

Date _____
Day _____
Time _____

Method & Supplementary Books	New Pages	Review Pages	Practice Suggestions
☐ Lesson Book			
☐ Theory Book			
☐ Recital or Solo Books			
☐ Notespeller Book			
☐ Technic Book			
☐ Activity & Ear Training Book			
☐			
☐			
☐			
Sheet Music Solos, Duets & Ensembles			
☐			
☐			

Daily Practice Time (in minutes)

SUN	MON	TUES	WED	THURS	FRI	SAT	TOTAL

Note from Teacher to Student or Parent:

....
....
....
....
....
....

Note from Parent or Student to Teacher:

....
....
....
....
....
....

Assignment
For Next Lesson

Date_____
Day _____
Time_____

Today's Lesson

Date _____
Day _____
Time _____

Method & Supplementary Books	New Pages	Review Pages	Practice Suggestions
☐ Lesson Book			
☐ Theory Book			
☐ Recital or Solo Books			
☐ Notespeller Book			
☐ Technic Book			
☐ Activity & Ear Training Book			
☐			
☐			
☐			
Sheet Music Solos, Duets & Ensembles			
☐			
☐			

Daily Practice Time (in minutes)

SUN	MON	TUES	WED	THURS	FRI	SAT	TOTAL

Note from Teacher to Student or Parent:

....
....
....
....
....

Note from Parent or Student to Teacher:

....
....
....
....
....

Assignment
For Next Lesson

Date_____
Day _____
Time_____

Today's Lesson

Date _____
Day _____
Time _____

Method & Supplementary Books	New Pages	Review Pages	Practice Suggestions
☐ Lesson Book			
☐ Theory Book			
☐ Recital or Solo Books			
☐ Notespeller Book			
☐ Technic Book			
☐ Activity & Ear Training Book			
☐			
☐			
☐			
Sheet Music Solos, Duets & Ensembles			
☐			
☐			

Daily Practice Time (in minutes)

SUN	MON	TUES	WED	THURS	FRI	SAT	TOTAL

Note from Teacher to Student or Parent:

....
....
....
....
....
....

Note from Parent or Student to Teacher:

....
....
....
....
....
....

Assignment
For Next Lesson

Date_____
Day _____
Time_____

Today's Lesson

Date _____
Day _____
Time _____

Method & Supplementary Books	New Pages	Review Pages	Practice Suggestions
☐ Lesson Book			
☐ Theory Book			
☐ Recital or Solo Books			
☐ Notespeller Book			
☐ Technic Book			
☐ Activity & Ear Training Book			
☐			
☐			
☐			
Sheet Music Solos, Duets & Ensembles			
☐			
☐			

Daily Practice Time (in minutes)

SUN	MON	TUES	WED	THURS	FRI	SAT	**TOTAL**

Note from Teacher to Student or Parent:

....
....
....
....
....
....

Note from Parent or Student to Teacher:

....
....
....
....
....
....

Assignment
For Next Lesson

Date _____
Day _____
Time _____

Today's Lesson

Date _____
Day _____
Time _____

Method & Supplementary Books	New Pages	Review Pages	Practice Suggestions
☐ Lesson Book			....
			....
☐ Theory Book			....
☐ Recital or Solo Books			....
☐ Notespeller Book			....
☐ Technic Book			....
☐ Activity & Ear Training Book			....
☐			....
☐			....
☐			....
Sheet Music Solos, Duets & Ensembles			....
☐			....
☐			....

Daily Practice Time (in minutes)

SUN	MON	TUES	WED	THURS	FRI	SAT	**TOTAL**

Note from Teacher to Student or Parent:

....
....
....
....
....

Note from Parent or Student to Teacher:

....
....
....
....
....

Assignment

For Next Lesson

Date _____
Day _____
Time _____

Today's Lesson

Date _____
Day _____
Time _____

Method & Supplementary Books	New Pages	Review Pages	Practice Suggestions
☐ Lesson Book			....
			....
☐ Theory Book			....
☐ Recital or Solo Books			....
☐ Notespeller Book			....
☐ Technic Book			....
☐ Activity & Ear Training Book			....
☐			....
☐			....
☐			....
Sheet Music Solos, Duets & Ensembles			....
☐			....
☐			....

Daily Practice Time (in minutes)

SUN	MON	TUES	WED	THURS	FRI	SAT	TOTAL

Note from Teacher to Student or Parent:

....
....
....
....
....

Note from Parent or Student to Teacher:

....
....
....
....
....

Assignment
For Next Lesson

Date _____
Day _____
Time _____

Today's Lesson

Date _____
Day _____
Time _____

Method & Supplementary Books	New Pages	Review Pages	Practice Suggestions
☐ Lesson Book			
☐ Theory Book			
☐ Recital or Solo Books			
☐ Notespeller Book			
☐ Technic Book			
☐ Activity & Ear Training Book			
☐			
☐			
☐			
Sheet Music Solos, Duets & Ensembles			
☐			
☐			

Daily Practice Time (in minutes)

SUN	MON	TUES	WED	THURS	FRI	SAT	TOTAL

Note from Teacher to Student or Parent:

....
....
....
....
....

Note from Parent or Student to Teacher:

....
....
....
....
....

Assignment
For Next Lesson

Date _____
Day _____
Time _____

Today's Lesson

Date _____
Day _____
Time _____

Method & Supplementary Books	New Pages	Review Pages	Practice Suggestions
☐ Lesson Book			
☐ Theory Book			
☐ Recital or Solo Books			
☐ Notespeller Book			
☐ Technic Book			
☐ Activity & Ear Training Book			
☐			
☐			
☐			
Sheet Music Solos, Duets & Ensembles			
☐			
☐			

Daily Practice Time (in minutes)

SUN	MON	TUES	WED	THURS	FRI	SAT	**TOTAL**

Note from Teacher to Student or Parent:

....
....
....
....
....

Note from Parent or Student to Teacher:

....
....
....
....
....

Assignment
For Next Lesson

Date_____
Day _____
Time_____

Today's Lesson

Date _____
Day _____
Time _____

Method & Supplementary Books	New Pages	Review Pages	Practice Suggestions
☐ Lesson Book			....
			....
☐ Theory Book			....
☐ Recital or Solo Books			....
☐ Notespeller Book			....
☐ Technic Book			....
☐ Activity & Ear Training Book			....
☐			....
☐			....
☐			....
Sheet Music Solos, Duets & Ensembles			....
☐			....
☐			....

Daily Practice Time (in minutes)

SUN	MON	TUES	WED	THURS	FRI	SAT	TOTAL

Note from Teacher to Student or Parent:

....
....
....
....
....
....

Note from Parent or Student to Teacher:

....
....
....
....
....
....

Assignment
For Next Lesson

Date _____
Day _____
Time _____

Today's Lesson

Date _____
Day _____
Time _____

Method & Supplementary Books	New Pages	Review Pages	Practice Suggestions
☐ Lesson Book			
☐ Theory Book			
☐ Recital or Solo Books			
☐ Notespeller Book			
☐ Technic Book			
☐ Activity & Ear Training Book			
☐			
☐			
☐			
Sheet Music Solos, Duets & Ensembles			
☐			
☐			

Daily Practice Time (in minutes)

SUN	MON	TUES	WED	THURS	FRI	SAT	TOTAL

Note from Teacher to Student or Parent:

....
....
....
....
....
....

Note from Parent or Student to Teacher:

....
....
....
....
....
....

Assignment
For Next Lesson

Date _____
Day _____
Time _____

Today's Lesson

Date _____
Day _____
Time _____

Method & Supplementary Books	New Pages	Review Pages	Practice Suggestions
☐ Lesson Book			....
			....
☐ Theory Book			....
☐ Recital or Solo Books			....
☐ Notespeller Book			....
☐ Technic Book			....
☐ Activity & Ear Training Book			....
☐			....
☐			....
☐			....
Sheet Music Solos, Duets & Ensembles			....
☐			....
☐			....

Daily Practice Time (in minutes)

SUN	MON	TUES	WED	THURS	FRI	SAT	TOTAL

Note from Teacher to Student or Parent:

....
....
....
....
....
....

Note from Parent or Student to Teacher:

....
....
....
....
....
....

Assignment
For Next Lesson

Date _____
Day _____
Time _____

Today's Lesson

Date _____
Day _____
Time _____

Method & Supplementary Books	New Pages	Review Pages	Practice Suggestions
☐ Lesson Book			--------------------------

☐ Theory Book			--------------------------
☐ Recital or Solo Books			--------------------------
☐ Notespeller Book			--------------------------
☐ Technic Book			--------------------------
☐ Activity & Ear Training Book			--------------------------
☐			--------------------------
☐			--------------------------
☐			--------------------------
Sheet Music Solos, Duets & Ensembles			--------------------------
☐			--------------------------
☐			--------------------------

Daily Practice Time (in minutes)

SUN	MON	TUES	WED	THURS	FRI	SAT	TOTAL

Note from Teacher to Student or Parent:

....
....
....
....
....
....

Note from Parent or Student to Teacher:

....
....
....
....
....
....

Assignment
For Next Lesson

Date _____
Day _____
Time _____

Today's Lesson

Date _____
Day _____
Time _____

Method & Supplementary Books	New Pages	Review Pages	Practice Suggestions
☐ Lesson Book			....
			....
☐ Theory Book			....
☐ Recital or Solo Books			....
☐ Notespeller Book			....
☐ Technic Book			....
☐ Activity & Ear Training Book			....
☐			....
☐			....
☐			....
Sheet Music Solos, Duets & Ensembles			....
☐			....
☐			....

Daily Practice Time (in minutes)

SUN	MON	TUES	WED	THURS	FRI	SAT	**TOTAL**

Note from Teacher to Student or Parent:

....
....
....
....
....
....

Note from Parent or Student to Teacher:

....
....
....
....
....
....

Assignment
For Next Lesson

Date_____
Day _____
Time_____

Today's Lesson

Date _____
Day _____
Time _____

Method & Supplementary Books	New Pages	Review Pages	Practice Suggestions
☐ Lesson Book			....
			....
☐ Theory Book			....
☐ Recital or Solo Books			....
☐ Notespeller Book			....
☐ Technic Book			....
☐ Activity & Ear Training Book			....
☐			....
☐			....
☐			....
Sheet Music Solos, Duets & Ensembles			....
☐			....
☐			....

Daily Practice Time (in minutes)

SUN	MON	TUES	WED	THURS	FRI	SAT	**TOTAL**

Note from Teacher to Student or Parent:

....
....
....
....
....
....

Note from Parent or Student to Teacher:

....
....
....
....
....
....

Assignment
For Next Lesson

Date _____
Day _____
Time _____

Today's Lesson

Date _____

Day _____

Time _____

Method & Supplementary Books	New Pages	Review Pages	Practice Suggestions
☐ Lesson Book			-------------------------------

☐ Theory Book			-------------------------------
☐ Recital or Solo Books			-------------------------------
☐ Notespeller Book			-------------------------------
☐ Technic Book			-------------------------------
☐ Activity & Ear Training Book			-------------------------------
☐			-------------------------------
☐			-------------------------------
☐			-------------------------------
Sheet Music Solos, Duets & Ensembles			-------------------------------
☐			-------------------------------
☐			-------------------------------

Daily Practice Time (in minutes)

SUN	MON	TUES	WED	THURS	FRI	SAT	TOTAL

Note from Teacher to Student or Parent:

....
....
....
....
....
....

Note from Parent or Student to Teacher:

....
....
....
....
....
....

Assignment
For Next Lesson

Date _____
Day _____
Time _____

Today's Lesson

Date _____
Day _____
Time _____

Method & Supplementary Books	New Pages	Review Pages	Practice Suggestions
☐ Lesson Book			
☐ Theory Book			
☐ Recital or Solo Books			
☐ Notespeller Book			
☐ Technic Book			
☐ Activity & Ear Training Book			
☐			
☐			
☐			
Sheet Music Solos, Duets & Ensembles			
☐			
☐			

Daily Practice Time (in minutes)

SUN	MON	TUES	WED	THURS	FRI	SAT	TOTAL

Note from Teacher to Student or Parent:

....

....

....

....

....

....

Note from Parent or Student to Teacher:

....

....

....

....

....

....

Assignment
For Next Lesson

Date_____
Day _____
Time_____

Today's Lesson

Date _____
Day _____
Time _____

Method & Supplementary Books	New Pages	Review Pages	Practice Suggestions
☐ Lesson Book			....
			....
☐ Theory Book			....
☐ Recital or Solo Books			....
☐ Notespeller Book			....
☐ Technic Book			....
☐ Activity & Ear Training Book			....
☐			....
☐			....
☐			....
Sheet Music Solos, Duets & Ensembles			....
☐			....
☐			....

Daily Practice Time (in minutes)

SUN	MON	TUES	WED	THURS	FRI	SAT	TOTAL

Note from Teacher to Student or Parent:

....
....
....
....
....

Note from Parent or Student to Teacher:

....
....
....
....
....

Assignment
For Next Lesson

Date _____
Day _____
Time _____

Today's Lesson

Date _____
Day _____
Time _____

Method & Supplementary Books	New Pages	Review Pages	Practice Suggestions
☐ Lesson Book			-------------------

☐ Theory Book			-------------------
☐ Recital or Solo Books			-------------------
☐ Notespeller Book			-------------------
☐ Technic Book			-------------------
☐ Activity & Ear Training Book			-------------------
☐			-------------------
☐			-------------------
☐			-------------------
Sheet Music Solos, Duets & Ensembles			-------------------
☐			-------------------
☐			-------------------

Daily Practice Time (in minutes)

SUN	MON	TUES	WED	THURS	FRI	SAT	**TOTAL**

Note from Teacher to Student or Parent:

....
....
....
....
....
....

Note from Parent or Student to Teacher:

....
....
....
....
....
....

Assignment
For Next Lesson

Date _____
Day _____
Time _____

Today's Lesson

Date _____
Day _____
Time _____

Method & Supplementary Books	New Pages	Review Pages	Practice Suggestions
☐ Lesson Book			------------------------------

☐ Theory Book			------------------------------
☐ Recital or Solo Books			------------------------------
☐ Notespeller Book			------------------------------
☐ Technic Book			------------------------------
☐ Activity & Ear Training Book			------------------------------
☐			------------------------------
☐			------------------------------
☐			------------------------------
Sheet Music Solos, Duets & Ensembles			------------------------------
☐			------------------------------
☐			------------------------------

Daily Practice Time (in minutes)

SUN	MON	TUES	WED	THURS	FRI	SAT	**TOTAL**

Note from Teacher to Student or Parent:

....

....

....

....

....

....

Note from Parent or Student to Teacher:

....

....

....

....

....

....

Assignment
For Next Lesson

Date_____
Day _____
Time_____

Today's Lesson

Date _____
Day _____
Time _____

Method & Supplementary Books	New Pages	Review Pages	Practice Suggestions
☐ Lesson Book			....
			....
☐ Theory Book			....
☐ Recital or Solo Books			....
☐ Notespeller Book			....
☐ Technic Book			....
☐ Activity & Ear Training Book			....
☐			....
☐			....
☐			....
Sheet Music Solos, Duets & Ensembles			....
☐			....
☐			....

Daily Practice Time (in minutes)

SUN	MON	TUES	WED	THURS	FRI	SAT	**TOTAL**

Note from Teacher to Student or Parent:

....
....
....
....
....
....

Note from Parent or Student to Teacher:

....
....
....
....
....
....

Assignment
For Next Lesson

Date _____
Day _____
Time _____

Today's Lesson

Date _____
Day _____
Time _____

Method & Supplementary Books	New Pages	Review Pages	Practice Suggestions
☐ Lesson Book			
☐ Theory Book			
☐ Recital or Solo Books			
☐ Notespeller Book			
☐ Technic Book			
☐ Activity & Ear Training Book			
☐			
☐			
☐			
Sheet Music Solos, Duets & Ensembles			
☐			
☐			

Daily Practice Time (in minutes)

SUN	MON	TUES	WED	THURS	FRI	SAT	**TOTAL**

Note from Teacher to Student or Parent:

....
....
....
....
....
....

Note from Parent or Student to Teacher:

....
....
....
....
....
....

Assignment
For Next Lesson

Date _____
Day _____
Time _____

Today's Lesson

Date _____
Day _____
Time _____

Method & Supplementary Books	New Pages	Review Pages	Practice Suggestions
☐ Lesson Book			....
			....
☐ Theory Book			....
☐ Recital or Solo Books			....
☐ Notespeller Book			....
☐ Technic Book			....
☐ Activity & Ear Training Book			....
☐			....
☐			....
☐			....
Sheet Music Solos, Duets & Ensembles			....
☐			....
☐			....

Daily Practice Time (in minutes)

SUN	MON	TUES	WED	THURS	FRI	SAT	TOTAL

Note from Teacher to Student or Parent:

....
....
....
....
....
....

Note from Parent or Student to Teacher:

....
....
....
....
....
....

Assignment
For Next Lesson

Date _____
Day _____
Time _____

Today's Lesson

Date _____
Day _____
Time _____

Method & Supplementary Books	New Pages	Review Pages	Practice Suggestions
☐ Lesson Book			....
			....
☐ Theory Book			....
☐ Recital or Solo Books			....
☐ Notespeller Book			....
☐ Technic Book			....
☐ Activity & Ear Training Book			....
☐			....
☐			....
☐			....
Sheet Music Solos, Duets & Ensembles			....
☐			....
☐			....

Daily Practice Time (in minutes)

SUN	MON	TUES	WED	THURS	FRI	SAT	TOTAL

Note from Teacher to Student or Parent:

....
....
....
....
....
....

Note from Parent or Student to Teacher:

....
....
....
....
....
....

Assignment
For Next Lesson

Date_____
Day_____
Time_____

Today's Lesson

Date _____
Day _____
Time _____

Method & Supplementary Books	New Pages	Review Pages	Practice Suggestions
☐ Lesson Book			....
			....
☐ Theory Book			....
☐ Recital or Solo Books			....
☐ Notespeller Book			....
☐ Technic Book			....
☐ Activity & Ear Training Book			....
☐			....
☐			....
☐			....
Sheet Music Solos, Duets & Ensembles			....
☐			....
☐			....

Daily Practice Time (in minutes)

SUN	MON	TUES	WED	THURS	FRI	SAT	TOTAL

Note from Teacher to Student or Parent:

....
....
....
....
....
....

Note from Parent or Student to Teacher:

....
....
....
....
....
....

Assignment
For Next Lesson

Date _____
Day _____
Time _____

Today's Lesson

Date _____
Day _____
Time _____

Method & Supplementary Books	New Pages	Review Pages	Practice Suggestions
☐ Lesson Book			-------------------------------

☐ Theory Book			-------------------------------
☐ Recital or Solo Books			-------------------------------
☐ Notespeller Book			-------------------------------
☐ Technic Book			-------------------------------
☐ Activity & Ear Training Book			-------------------------------
☐			-------------------------------
☐			-------------------------------
☐			-------------------------------
Sheet Music Solos, Duets & Ensembles			-------------------------------
☐			-------------------------------
☐			-------------------------------

Daily Practice Time (in minutes)

SUN	MON	TUES	WED	THURS	FRI	SAT	TOTAL

Note from Teacher to Student or Parent:

....
....
....
....
....
....

Note from Parent or Student to Teacher:

....
....
....
....
....
....

Assignment
For Next Lesson

Date _____
Day _____
Time _____

Today's Lesson

Date _____
Day _____
Time _____

Method & Supplementary Books	New Pages	Review Pages	Practice Suggestions
☐ Lesson Book			....
			....
☐ Theory Book			....
☐ Recital or Solo Books			....
☐ Notespeller Book			....
☐ Technic Book			....
☐ Activity & Ear Training Book			....
☐			....
☐			....
☐			....
Sheet Music Solos, Duets & Ensembles			....
☐			....
☐			....

Daily Practice Time (in minutes)

SUN	MON	TUES	WED	THURS	FRI	SAT	TOTAL

Note from Teacher to Student or Parent:

....
....
....
....
....
....

Note from Parent or Student to Teacher:

....
....
....
....
....
....

Assignment
For Next Lesson

Date _____
Day _____
Time _____

Today's Lesson

Date _____
Day _____
Time _____

Method & Supplementary Books	New Pages	Review Pages	Practice Suggestions
☐ Lesson Book			
☐ Theory Book			
☐ Recital or Solo Books			
☐ Notespeller Book			
☐ Technic Book			
☐ Activity & Ear Training Book			
☐			
☐			
☐			
Sheet Music Solos, Duets & Ensembles			
☐			
☐			

Daily Practice Time (in minutes)

SUN	MON	TUES	WED	THURS	FRI	SAT	TOTAL

Note from Teacher to Student or Parent:

....
....
....
....
....
....

Note from Parent or Student to Teacher:

....
....
....
....
....
....

Assignment
For Next Lesson

Date _____
Day _____
Time _____

Today's Lesson

Date _____
Day _____
Time _____

Method & Supplementary Books	New Pages	Review Pages	Practice Suggestions
☐ Lesson Book			
☐ Theory Book			
☐ Recital or Solo Books			
☐ Notespeller Book			
☐ Technic Book			
☐ Activity & Ear Training Book			
☐			
☐			
☐			
Sheet Music Solos, Duets & Ensembles			
☐			
☐			

Daily Practice Time (in minutes)

SUN	MON	TUES	WED	THURS	FRI	SAT	TOTAL

Note from Teacher to Student or Parent:

....

....

....

....

....

Note from Parent or Student to Teacher:

....

....

....

....

....

Assignment
For Next Lesson

Date _____
Day _____
Time _____

Today's Lesson

Date _____
Day _____
Time _____

Method & Supplementary Books	New Pages	Review Pages	Practice Suggestions
☐ Lesson Book			----------------------

☐ Theory Book			----------------------
☐ Recital or Solo Books			----------------------
☐ Notespeller Book			----------------------
☐ Technic Book			----------------------
☐ Activity & Ear Training Book			----------------------
☐			----------------------
☐			----------------------
☐			----------------------
Sheet Music Solos, Duets & Ensembles			----------------------
☐			----------------------
☐			----------------------

Daily Practice Time (in minutes)

SUN	MON	TUES	WED	THURS	FRI	SAT	TOTAL

Note from Teacher to Student or Parent:

....
....
....
....
....
....

Note from Parent or Student to Teacher:

....
....
....
....
....
....

Assignment
For Next Lesson

Date _____
Day _____
Time _____

Today's Lesson

Date _____
Day _____
Time _____

Method & Supplementary Books	New Pages	Review Pages	Practice Suggestions
☐ Lesson Book			....
			....
☐ Theory Book			....
☐ Recital or Solo Books			....
☐ Notespeller Book			....
☐ Technic Book			....
☐ Activity & Ear Training Book			....
☐			....
☐			....
☐			....
Sheet Music Solos, Duets & Ensembles			....
☐			....
☐			....

Daily Practice Time (in minutes)

SUN	MON	TUES	WED	THURS	FRI	SAT	TOTAL

Note from Teacher to Student or Parent:

....

....

....

....

....

....

Note from Parent or Student to Teacher:

....

....

....

....

....

....

Assignment
For Next Lesson

Date _____
Day _____
Time _____

Today's Lesson

Date _____
Day _____
Time _____

Method & Supplementary Books	New Pages	Review Pages	Practice Suggestions
☐ Lesson Book			
☐ Theory Book			
☐ Recital or Solo Books			
☐ Notespeller Book			
☐ Technic Book			
☐ Activity & Ear Training Book			
☐			
☐			
☐			
Sheet Music Solos, Duets & Ensembles			
☐			
☐			

Daily Practice Time (in minutes)

SUN	MON	TUES	WED	THURS	FRI	SAT	TOTAL

Note from Teacher to Student or Parent:

....
....
....
....
....
....

Note from Parent or Student to Teacher:

....
....
....
....
....
....

Assignment
For Next Lesson

Date _____
Day _____
Time _____

Today's Lesson

Date _____
Day _____
Time _____

Method & Supplementary Books	New Pages	Review Pages	Practice Suggestions
☐ Lesson Book			--------------------

☐ Theory Book			--------------------
☐ Recital or Solo Books			--------------------
☐ Notespeller Book			--------------------
☐ Technic Book			--------------------
☐ Activity & Ear Training Book			--------------------
☐			--------------------
☐			--------------------
☐			--------------------
Sheet Music Solos, Duets & Ensembles			--------------------
☐			--------------------
☐			--------------------

Daily Practice Time (in minutes)

SUN	MON	TUES	WED	THURS	FRI	SAT	TOTAL

Note from Teacher to Student or Parent:

....
....
....
....
....
....

Note from Parent or Student to Teacher:

....
....
....
....
....
....

Assignment
For Next Lesson

Date _____
Day _____
Time _____

Today's Lesson

Date _____
Day _____
Time _____

Method & Supplementary Books	New Pages	Review Pages	Practice Suggestions
☐ Lesson Book			-------------------------------------

☐ Theory Book			-------------------------------------
☐ Recital or Solo Books			-------------------------------------
☐ Notespeller Book			-------------------------------------
☐ Technic Book			-------------------------------------
☐ Activity & Ear Training Book			-------------------------------------
☐			-------------------------------------
☐			-------------------------------------
☐			-------------------------------------
Sheet Music Solos, Duets & Ensembles			-------------------------------------
☐			-------------------------------------
☐			-------------------------------------

Daily Practice Time (in minutes)

SUN	MON	TUES	WED	THURS	FRI	SAT	TOTAL

Note from Teacher to Student or Parent:

....

....

....

....

....

....

Note from Parent or Student to Teacher:

....

....

....

....

....

....

Assignment
For Next Lesson

Date_____
Day _____
Time_____

Today's Lesson

Date _____
Day _____
Time _____

Method & Supplementary Books	New Pages	Review Pages	Practice Suggestions
☐ Lesson Book			-------------------

☐ Theory Book			-------------------
☐ Recital or Solo Books			-------------------
☐ Notespeller Book			-------------------
☐ Technic Book			-------------------
☐ Activity & Ear Training Book			-------------------
☐			-------------------
☐			-------------------
☐			-------------------
Sheet Music Solos, Duets & Ensembles			-------------------
☐			-------------------
☐			-------------------

Daily Practice Time (in minutes)

SUN	MON	TUES	WED	THURS	FRI	SAT	TOTAL

Note from Teacher to Student or Parent:

....
....
....
....
....
....

Note from Parent or Student to Teacher:

....
....
....
....
....
....

Assignment
For Next Lesson

Date_____
Day _____
Time_____

Today's Lesson

Date _____
Day _____
Time_____

Method & Supplementary Books	New Pages	Review Pages	Practice Suggestions
☐ Lesson Book			
☐ Theory Book			
☐ Recital or Solo Books			
☐ Notespeller Book			
☐ Technic Book			
☐ Activity & Ear Training Book			
☐			
☐			
☐			
Sheet Music Solos, Duets & Ensembles			
☐			
☐			

Daily Practice Time (in minutes)

SUN	MON	TUES	WED	THURS	FRI	SAT	TOTAL

Note from Teacher to Student or Parent:

....

....

....

....

....

....

Note from Parent or Student to Teacher:

....

....

....

....

....

....

Assignment
For Next Lesson

Date_____
Day _____
Time_____

Today's Lesson

Date _____
Day _____
Time _____

Method & Supplementary Books	New Pages	Review Pages	Practice Suggestions
☐ Lesson Book			- - - - - - - - - - - - - - - -
			- - - - - - - - - - - - - - - -
☐ Theory Book			- - - - - - - - - - - - - - - -
☐ Recital or Solo Books			- - - - - - - - - - - - - - - -
☐ Notespeller Book			- - - - - - - - - - - - - - - -
☐ Technic Book			- - - - - - - - - - - - - - - -
☐ Activity & Ear Training Book			- - - - - - - - - - - - - - - -
☐			- - - - - - - - - - - - - - - -
☐			- - - - - - - - - - - - - - - -
☐			- - - - - - - - - - - - - - - -
Sheet Music Solos, Duets & Ensembles			- - - - - - - - - - - - - - - -
☐			- - - - - - - - - - - - - - - -
☐			- - - - - - - - - - - - - - - -

Daily Practice Time (in minutes)

SUN	MON	TUES	WED	THURS	FRI	SAT	TOTAL

Note from Teacher to Student or Parent:

....
....
....
....
....
....

Note from Parent or Student to Teacher:

....
....
....
....
....
....

Assignment
For Next Lesson

Date_____
Day _____
Time_____

Today's Lesson

Date _____
Day _____
Time _____

Method & Supplementary Books	New Pages	Review Pages	Practice Suggestions
☐ Lesson Book			--
			--
☐ Theory Book			--
☐ Recital or Solo Books			--
☐ Notespeller Book			--
☐ Technic Book			--
☐ Activity & Ear Training Book			--
☐			--
☐			--
☐			--
Sheet Music Solos, Duets & Ensembles			--
☐			--
☐			--

Daily Practice Time (in minutes)

SUN	MON	TUES	WED	THURS	FRI	SAT	TOTAL

Note from Teacher to Student or Parent:

....

....

....

....

....

....

Note from Parent or Student to Teacher:

....

....

....

....

....

....

Assignment
For Next Lesson

Date_____
Day _____
Time_____

Today's Lesson

Date _____
Day _____
Time _____

Method & Supplementary Books	New Pages	Review Pages	Practice Suggestions
☐ Lesson Book			--------------------------------

☐ Theory Book			--------------------------------
☐ Recital or Solo Books			--------------------------------
☐ Notespeller Book			--------------------------------
☐ Technic Book			--------------------------------
☐ Activity & Ear Training Book			--------------------------------
☐			--------------------------------
☐			--------------------------------
☐			--------------------------------
Sheet Music Solos, Duets & Ensembles			--------------------------------
☐			--------------------------------
☐			

Daily Practice Time (in minutes)

SUN	MON	TUES	WED	THURS	FRI	SAT	TOTAL

Note from Teacher to Student or Parent:

Note from Parent or Student to Teacher:

Assignment
For Next Lesson

Date _____
Day _____
Time _____

Today's Lesson

Date _____
Day _____
Time _____

Method & Supplementary Books	New Pages	Review Pages	Practice Suggestions
☐ Lesson Book			----------------------------

☐ Theory Book			----------------------------
☐ Recital or Solo Books			----------------------------
☐ Notespeller Book			----------------------------
☐ Technic Book			----------------------------
☐ Activity & Ear Training Book			----------------------------
☐			----------------------------
☐			----------------------------
☐			----------------------------
Sheet Music Solos, Duets & Ensembles			----------------------------
☐			----------------------------
☐			----------------------------

Daily Practice Time (in minutes)

SUN	MON	TUES	WED	THURS	FRI	SAT	TOTAL

Note from Teacher to Student or Parent:

....
....
....
....
....
....

Note from Parent or Student to Teacher:

....
....
....
....
....
....

Assignment
For Next Lesson

Date _____
Day _____
Time _____

Today's Lesson

Date _____
Day _____
Time _____

Method & Supplementary Books	New Pages	Review Pages	Practice Suggestions
☐ Lesson Book			------------------------------

☐ Theory Book			------------------------------
☐ Recital or Solo Books			------------------------------
☐ Notespeller Book			------------------------------
☐ Technic Book			------------------------------
☐ Activity & Ear Training Book			------------------------------
☐			------------------------------
☐			------------------------------
☐			------------------------------
Sheet Music Solos, Duets & Ensembles			------------------------------
☐			------------------------------
☐			------------------------------

Daily Practice Time (in minutes)

SUN	MON	TUES	WED	THURS	FRI	SAT	TOTAL

Note from Teacher to Student or Parent:

....
....
....
....
....
....

Note from Parent or Student to Teacher:

....
....
....
....
....
....

Assignment
For Next Lesson

Date_____
Day _____
Time_____

Today's Lesson

Date _____
Day _____
Time_____

Method & Supplementary Books	New Pages	Review Pages	Practice Suggestions
☐ Lesson Book			....
			....
☐ Theory Book			....
☐ Recital or Solo Books			....
☐ Notespeller Book			....
☐ Technic Book			....
☐ Activity & Ear Training Book			....
☐			....
☐			....
☐			....
Sheet Music Solos, Duets & Ensembles			....
☐			....
☐			....

Daily Practice Time (in minutes)

SUN	MON	TUES	WED	THURS	FRI	SAT	**TOTAL**

Note from Teacher to Student or Parent:

....

....

....

....

....

Note from Parent or Student to Teacher:

....

....

....

....

....

Assignment

For Next Lesson

Date _____
Day _____
Time _____

Today's Lesson

Date _____
Day _____
Time _____

Method & Supplementary Books	New Pages	Review Pages	Practice Suggestions
☐ Lesson Book			-------------------------------

☐ Theory Book			-------------------------------
☐ Recital or Solo Books			-------------------------------
☐ Notespeller Book			-------------------------------
☐ Technic Book			-------------------------------
☐ Activity & Ear Training Book			-------------------------------
☐			-------------------------------
☐			-------------------------------
☐			-------------------------------
Sheet Music Solos, Duets & Ensembles			-------------------------------
☐			-------------------------------
☐			-------------------------------

Daily Practice Time (in minutes)

SUN	MON	TUES	WED	THURS	FRI	SAT	TOTAL

Note from Teacher to Student or Parent:

....

....

....

....

....

....

Note from Parent or Student to Teacher:

....

....

....

....

....

....

Assignment
For Next Lesson

Date _____
Day _____
Time _____

Today's Lesson

Date _____

Day _____

Time _____

Method & Supplementary Books	New Pages	Review Pages	Practice Suggestions
☐ Lesson Book			------------------------------------

☐ Theory Book			------------------------------------
☐ Recital or Solo Books			------------------------------------
☐ Notespeller Book			------------------------------------
☐ Technic Book			------------------------------------
☐ Activity & Ear Training Book			------------------------------------
☐			------------------------------------
☐			------------------------------------
☐			------------------------------------
Sheet Music Solos, Duets & Ensembles			------------------------------------
☐			------------------------------------
☐			------------------------------------

Daily Practice Time (in minutes)

SUN	MON	TUES	WED	THURS	FRI	SAT	TOTAL

Note from Teacher to Student or Parent:

....

....

....

....

....

....

Note from Parent or Student to Teacher:

....

....

....

....

....

....

Assignment
For Next Lesson

Date _____
Day _____
Time _____

Today's Lesson

Date _____
Day _____
Time _____

Method & Supplementary Books	New Pages	Review Pages	Practice Suggestions
☐ Lesson Book			
☐ Theory Book			
☐ Recital or Solo Books			
☐ Notespeller Book			
☐ Technic Book			
☐ Activity & Ear Training Book			
☐			
☐			
☐			
Sheet Music Solos, Duets & Ensembles			
☐			
☐			

Daily Practice Time (in minutes)

SUN	MON	TUES	WED	THURS	FRI	SAT	**TOTAL**

Note from Teacher to Student or Parent:

....

....

....

....

....

....

Note from Parent or Student to Teacher:

....

....

....

....

....

....

Assignment
For Next Lesson

Date_____
Day _____
Time_____

Today's Lesson

Date _____

Day _____

Time _____

Method & Supplementary Books	New Pages	Review Pages	Practice Suggestions
☐ Lesson Book			
☐ Theory Book			
☐ Recital or Solo Books			
☐ Notespeller Book			
☐ Technic Book			
☐ Activity & Ear Training Book			
☐			
☐			
☐			
Sheet Music Solos, Duets & Ensembles			
☐			
☐			

Daily Practice Time (in minutes)

SUN	MON	TUES	WED	THURS	FRI	SAT	TOTAL

Note from Teacher to Student or Parent:

....
....
....
....
....
....

Note from Parent or Student to Teacher:

....
....
....
....
....
....

<table>
<tr><td colspan="3">

Assignment
For Next Lesson

</td><td>

Date_____
Day _____
Time_____

</td><td>

Today's Lesson
Date _____
Day _____
Time _____

</td></tr>
</table>

Method & Supplementary Books	New Pages	Review Pages	Practice Suggestions
☐ Lesson Book			
☐ Theory Book			
☐ Recital or Solo Books			
☐ Notespeller Book			
☐ Technic Book			
☐ Activity & Ear Training Book			
☐			
☐			
☐			
Sheet Music Solos, Duets & Ensembles			
☐			
☐			

Daily Practice Time (in minutes)

SUN	MON	TUES	WED	THURS	FRI	SAT	TOTAL

Note from Teacher to Student or Parent:

....

....

....

....

....

....

Note from Parent or Student to Teacher:

....

....

....

....

....

....

Assignment
For Next Lesson

Date _____
Day _____
Time _____

Today's Lesson

Date _____
Day _____
Time _____

Method & Supplementary Books	New Pages	Review Pages	Practice Suggestions
☐ Lesson Book			- - - - - - - - - - - - - - - -
			- - - - - - - - - - - - - - - -
☐ Theory Book			- - - - - - - - - - - - - - - -
☐ Recital or Solo Books			- - - - - - - - - - - - - - - -
☐ Notespeller Book			- - - - - - - - - - - - - - - -
☐ Technic Book			- - - - - - - - - - - - - - - -
☐ Activity & Ear Training Book			- - - - - - - - - - - - - - - -
☐			- - - - - - - - - - - - - - - -
☐			- - - - - - - - - - - - - - - -
☐			- - - - - - - - - - - - - - - -
Sheet Music Solos, Duets & Ensembles			- - - - - - - - - - - - - - - -
☐			- - - - - - - - - - - - - - - -
☐			- - - - - - - - - - - - - - - -

Daily Practice Time (in minutes)

SUN	MON	TUES	WED	THURS	FRI	SAT	TOTAL

Note from Teacher to Student or Parent:

....
....
....
....
....
....

Note from Parent or Student to Teacher:

....
....
....
....
....
....

Assignment
For Next Lesson

Date _____
Day _____
Time _____

Today's Lesson

Date _____
Day _____
Time _____

Method & Supplementary Books	New Pages	Review Pages	Practice Suggestions
☐ Lesson Book			
☐ Theory Book			
☐ Recital or Solo Books			
☐ Notespeller Book			
☐ Technic Book			
☐ Activity & Ear Training Book			
☐			
☐			
☐			
Sheet Music Solos, Duets & Ensembles			
☐			
☐			

Daily Practice Time (in minutes)

SUN	MON	TUES	WED	THURS	FRI	SAT	TOTAL

Note from Teacher to Student or Parent:

....
....
....
....
....
....

Note from Parent or Student to Teacher:

....
....
....
....
....
....

Music I Have Memorized

Music Books & Pieces I Have Studied

Music Books

. . . .

. . . .

. . . .

. . . .

. . . .

. . . .

. . . .

. . . .

. . . .

. . . .

Sheet Music Solos, Duets and Ensembles

. . . .

. . . .

. . . .

. . . .

. . . .

. . . .

. . . .

. . . .

. . . .

Music I Have Performed

Piece	Date	Event
....	....	....
....	....	....
....	....	....
....	....	....
....	....	....
....	....	....
....	....	....
....	....	....
....	....	....
....	....	....
....	....	....
....	....	....
....	....	....
....	....	....
....	....	....
....	....	....
....	....	....
....	....	....
....	....	....
....	....	....

Music I Have Borrowed from My Teacher

Book/Piece	Date Borrowed	Date Returned

Alfred's Basic Prep Course • Level A

Lesson Book A With this page(s)	Theory Book A Use this page(s)	Solo Book A Use after page(s)	Notespeller Book A Use this page(s)	Technic Book A Use with page(s)	Activity & Ear Training Book A Use with page(s)
4 - How to Sit at the Piano	2-3				
5 - Fingers Have Numbers	4-5				3-4
6 - 2 Black Keys	6-7				5
7 - 3 Black Keys	8-9				6
8 - Left Hand Playing	10				7-8
9 - Right Hand Playing	11				9
10 - Sing Along!	12				10
11 - End of Song!	13				11
12 - Merrily We Roll Along					12
13 - O'er the Deep Blue Sea	14-15				13
14 - Hand-Bells (part 1 for left hand)	16				14
15 - Hand-Bells (part 2 for right hand)	17	4 - Teddy's Tuba, 5 - Polly's Piccolo			15
16 - A B C D E F G	18		2		16
17 - An Easy Way to Find any White Key	19		3		17
18 - A Mellow Melody	19		4	2	18
19 - A Happy Melody	20	6-7 - Fuzzy Wuzzy	5	3	19
20 - Come and Play!	20	8 - Dyno, My Pet Dinosaur	6		20
21 - Tongue-Twister	20	8 - Dyno, My Pet Dinosaur	7	4	20
22 - My Clever Pup	21-22	9 - Right, Left!	8	5	21
23 - Kitty Cat	23	9 - Right, Left!	9		22
24 - Roller Coaster	23		10	6	23
25 - The Zoo	24	10-11 - A Big Surprise!	11	7	24
26 - C Position	25		12	8	25
27 - For My Teacher!			13	9	26
28 - 29 - Sailing	26	12-13 - Come, Fly with Me!	14	10	27
30 - Wishing Well	27	12-13 - Come, Fly with Me!	15	11	28
31 - The Staff*	28		16-17		29
32 - The Bass Clef Sign	29		18		30
33 - Rain, Rain!	30-31		19	12	31
34 - Mrs. Murphy's House	30-31	14 - Candy Shopping	20	13	32
35 - Look at Me!	32	15 - Song of Joy	21	14	33
36 - The Treble Clef Sign	33		22		34
37 - A Happy Song	34-35		23	15	35
38 - Gee, We're Glad!	34-35	16 - A Little Smile	24	16	36
39 - Little Bird	34-35	17 - Music Box	25	17	37
40 - The Grand Staff*	36		26		38
41 - "Position C"	37	18 - C for Cat, 19 - G for Girl	27	18	39
42 - Morning Prayer	37	20 - I Like You	28	19	40
43 - A Funny, Sunny Day	38	20 - I Like You	29	20	41
44 - Christopher Columbus	39-40	21 - I Can Do It!	30	21	42
45 - What a Song!	39-40	22-23 - Carousel	31	22	43
46 - 47 Graduation Song	39-40	24 - Now I've Done It!	32	23	44

*In the Universal edition of Lesson Book A, some of the above titles have been changed: page 31 - The Stave, page 40 - The Grand Stave.

Lesson Book B With this page(s)	Theory Book B Use this page(s)	Solo Book B Use after page(s)	Notespeller Book B Use this page(s)	Technic Book B Use with page(s)	Activity & Ear Training Book B Use with page(s)
4 - Circus Day!	2-3		3		3
5 - Smoothly Rocking	4			2	4
6 - Row, Row, Row Your Boat	5		4		5
7 - Seconds	6-7		5		6
8 - Gliding	6-7	4 - Calendar Song		3	7
9 - Balloons	8-9	5 - Play a Little Samba!	6	4-5	8
10 - Play a Third!	10				9
11 - Come and Play!	11	6 - Puppies and Guppies	7	6	10
12 - Hot Dog!	11				11
13 - What Can We Do?	11	7 - Our Team	8	7	12
14 - More about Intervals	12-13		9		13
15 - Pop Song	12-13			8	14
16 - Taking Turns	14	8 - Chopsticks, Anyone?	10		15
17 - Quiet River	15			9	16
18 - Rockets	15	9 - If I Won Ten Million Dollars	11		17
19 - Sea Divers	15		12	10	18
20 - That's a Fourth	16		13		19
21 - Let's Have Fun!	17	10-11 - Penguins on Parade	14	11	20
22 - Love Somebody	17				21
23 - Showstopper!	18		15	12	22
24 - Where Did You Get That Hat?	19				23
25 - Growing Up!	19	12 - Music Makes Me Glad!	16	13	24
26 - That's a Fifth!	20		17	14	25
27 - What Will You Do?	21				26
28 - Airplanes	21	13 - Buy a Balloon!	18	15	27
29 - Little Things	21	14 - My Big Bass Drum			28
30 - "Position G"	22		19	16	29
31 - "Moon-Walk"	23	15 - Clowns!	20	17	30
32 - 33 - Jingle Bells!	24-25	16-17 - Tons of Fun!	21		31
34 - Boogie Woogie Beat!	26		22	18	32
35 - Make Time for Music!	27	18 - My Robot	23		33
36 - Rockin' Tune	28	19 - Television	24	19	34
37 - Marching Song	29	19 - Television	25		35
38 - Indian Song	30	20 - Si, Si, Si!	26		36
39 - Mumbo-Jumbo	31	20 - Si, Si, Si!	27	20	37
40 - Raindrops	32		28	21	38
41 - Cracker Jack!	33	21 - Popcorn Popping!	29		39
42 - Hide and Seek	34-35		30	22	40
43 - Anyone for Tic-Tac-Toe?	36-37	22-23 - I'm a Puppet!	31	23	41
44 - 45 - Celebration	38-39	24 - See You Later!	32		42
46 - 47 - Review	40				43-44

Lesson Book C With this page(s)	Theory Book C Use this page(s)	Solo Book C Use after page(s)	Notespeller Book C Use this page(s)	Technic Book C Use with page(s)	Activity & Ear Training Book C Use with page(s)
4 - Review	2-3		2		3
5 - Review	4-5		3		4
6 - Brother John	6-7		4	2	5
7 - Seaside Stroll	8-9	4-5 - Friendship!	5	3	6
8 - 9 - Money Can't Buy Ev'rything!	10-11	6-7 - Say "Cheese"	6	4	7-8
10 - G's in the BAG	12		7		9
11 - Let it Rain, Let it Pour	13	8 - Willie and Tillie	8	5	10
12 - 13 - Oom-Pa-Pa!	14-15		9	6	11-12
14 - The Clown	16-18	9 - Tambourine Dance	10	7	13-14
15 - A Friend Like You	19		11		15
16 - 17 - When the Saints Go Marching In	20	10-11 - My Bubble Gum Song	12	8	16
18 - Reading in Middle C Position	21-22		13		17
19 - Thumbs on C!	21-22		14	9	18
20 - 21 - My First Waltz	23		15	10	19-20
22 - 23 - Jolly Old Saint Nicholas	24	12 - A Little Prelude	16	11	21-22
24 - 25 - Twinkle, Twinkle, Little Star	25	13 - A Strange Story	17		23-24
26 - 27 - The Rainbow	26	14-15 - The Silent Forest	18	12	25-26
28 - Good Morning to You!			19		27
29 - Happy Birthday to You!	27-28	16-17 - The Bus Song	20	13	28
30 - 31 - Amazing Grace	29	18-19 - My Garden	21	14	29
32 - 33 - Old MacDonald	30-31		22	15	30
34 - 35 - I'm a Little Teapot	32-33	20-21 - Springtime Symphony	23	16	31
36 - 37 - Bingo	34	24 - Bourée*	24	17	32
38 - Little Green Frog	35		25	18	33
39 - Arioso	35		26	19	34
40 - Get Away!	36		27	20	35
41 - Bake Me a Pie	36	22 - Rock Anywhere!	28	21	36
42 - 43 - A Cowboy's Song	37-38	23 - The Elephant and the Flea	29	22	37-38
44 - 45 - Indians	39	24 - Bourrée (or after page 36)	30	23	39-40
46 - 47 - Review Test	40		31-32		41-42

* may be used anytime after page 36

Alfred's Basic Prep Course • Level D

Lesson Book D With this page(s)	Theory Book D Use this page(s)	Solo Book D Use after page(s)	Notespeller Book D Use this page(s)	Technic Book D Use with page(s)	Activity & Ear Training Book D Use with page(s)
4 - 5 The Magic Man	2	4-5 - I'm a Winner!	2	2	3
6 - Whoopee Ti-Yi-Yo	3	6-7 - Will You, Won't You?	3	3	4
7 - Rock It Away!	3	6-7 - Will You, Won't You?	4	3	5
8 - New Position G	4		5	4	6
9 - Can't Get 'Em Up!	5-6		6	4	7
10 - 11 - I've Been Wishin'	7-9	8-9 - Andy, the Android	7	5	8
12 - Für Ludwig	10		8	5	9
13 - Amigos	11		9	6 - Group 5A	10
14 - 15 My Computer	12-13	10-11 - A Little Swingin' Song	10	7 - Group 5B	11
16 - 17 Minuet and Trio	14-15	12-13 - The Inspector General	11	8-9	12-13
18 - Four Position March	16		12	10 - Group 7A	14
19 - Five Position Waltz	17	14-15 - Spanish Dancer	13	11 - Group 7B	15
20 - 21 - Blue and Low	18		14	12-13	16-17
22 - Pedal Play	19		15	14 - Group 9A	18
23 - Harp Song	20		15	15 - Group 9B	19
24 - 25 - A Concert Piece	21	16-17 - A Concert Waltz	16		20-21
26 - Measuring Half Steps	22-23		17	16 - Group 10A	22
27 - Rockin' Half Steps	22-23	18-19 - A Mystery Story	18		23
28 - 29 - Boogie-Woogie Goose	24	18-19 - A Mystery Story	19		24
30 - Preparation for The Planets	25		20	17 - Group 10B	25
31 - The Planets	26-27	20-21 - The Rings of Saturn	21		26
32 - 33 - What a Happy Day!	28		22	18 - Group 11*	27-28
34 - 35 - The Thing that Has No Name!	29		23		29-30
36 - Tetrachords	30-31		24	19	31
37 - The Major Scale	32-34		25-26	20 - Group 13A	32
38 - Carol in G Major	35			20 - Group 13B	33
39 - Three Wise Monkeys	35	22-23 - Noisy Toys	27	21	34
40 - 41 - The Mermaid	36-37	22-23 - Noisy Toys	28		35-36
42 - 43 - The Caravan	38	24 - The Purple Cow	29	22 - Group 15A	37
44 - 45 - The Baseball Game	39	24 - The Purple Cow	30	23 - Group 15B	38-39
46 - Ta-dah!	40		31		40
47 - Review of Musical Terms			32		41-42

* 11A with page 32.
11B with page 33.

Alfred's Basic Prep Course • Level E

Lesson Book E With this page(s)	Theory Book E Use this page(s)	Solo Book E Use after page(s)	Notespeller Book E Use this page(s)	Technic Book E Use with page(s)	Activity & Ear Training Book E Use with page(s)
4 - 5 - Favorite Words	2-3	4-5 - A Walk in Space	2	2	3
6 - 7 - Introducing Dotted Quarter Notes	4-5		3		4-5
8 - Alouette	6	6-7 - The Music Machine	4	3	6
9 - Pastorale	7	8 - Green Meadow	5		7
10 - Ode to Joy	8		6	4 - Group 3A	8
11 - Toymaker's Dance	9		7	4 - Group 3B	9
12 - Measuring 6ths	10		8	5 - Group 4A	10
13 - Lavender's Blue	11	9 - 18th Century Dance	9	5 - Group 4B	11
14 - When You Grow Up	12	10-11 - Bell Song	10	6 - Group 5A	12
15 - Kum-ba-yah!	13	12-13 - Rockin' on 6!	11	6 - Group 5B	13
16 - More about 6ths	14		12	7 - Group 6A	14
17 - Mary Ann	15	14 - Skip to My Lou	13	7 - Group 6B	15
18 - 19 - A Quiet Song	16-17	15 - Play with All Your Heart!	14	8	16
20 - 21 - Lone Star Waltz	18	16-17 - Come and Dance the Polka!	15	9	17
22 - Cathedral Bells	19		16	10	18
23 - London Bridge	20-21			11	19
24 - On the Bridge at Avignon					20
25 - Come, Thou Almighty King	22	18-19 - Fantastic Dance	17	12 - Group 11A	21
26 - 27 - Malagueña	23	20-21 - Samba Time!	18	12 - Group 11B	22
28 - Measuring 7ths	24		19	13 - Group 12A	23
29 - Our Special Waltz		22-23 - Nocturne	20	13 - Group 12B	24
30 - 31 - Theme from a Mozart Sonata	25	24-25 - New Sounds	21	14	25
32 - More About the Major Scale	26		22	15	26
33 - Prelude		26-27 - Etude in C	23	16	27
34 - 35 - Let Me Tell You 'Bout the Blues	27		24		28
36 - Measuring Octaves (8ths)	28		25	17	29
37 - The Can-Can		28-29 - Swiss Melody	26	18	30
38 - 39 - Whistlin' Sam	29		27		31
40 - More About the G Major Scale	30		28	19	32
41 - Arkansas Traveler		30 - Polka in G	29	20	33
42 - 43 - A Classical Moment	31	31 - The Galway Piper	30	21	34
44 - 45 - Allegro Giocoso	32	32 - Two-Part Invention	31	22-23	35
46 - 47 - Review Test			32		36-37

Alfred's Basic Prep Course • Level F

Lesson Book F With this page(s)	Theory Book F Use this page(s)	Solo Book F Use after page(s)	Notespeller Book F Use this page(s)	Technic Book F Use with page(s)	Activity & Ear Training Book F Use with page(s)
4 - 5 - It's Such a Super-Special Sorta Song!	2	4-5 - A Lazy Morning	2	2	3
6 - 7 - Melody with Ostinato	3	6-7 - Clementine	3		4
8 - 9 - Ragtime Man	4-5	8-9 - Wash-Day Boogie	4	3	5
10 - Triads	6		5	4	6
11 - Square Dance	6	10-11 - Hoe-Down!	6		7
12 - 13 - The Harmonica Player	7		7	5	8
14 - 15 - Cockles and Mussels	8	12-13 - Bourrée	8	6	9
16 - The Primary Triads / Chord Progressions	9-10		9	7	10
17 - Blue Scales	11		10	8	11
18 - The I and V7 Chords in C Major	12		11	9	12
19 - The Song That Never Ends!	13		12		13
20 - The Primary Chords in C Major	14		13-14	10	14-15
21 - Got Lotsa Rhythm!	15			11 - Group 10A	16
22 - 23 - This Song!	16	14-15 - Look at Me! I'm Dancin'!	15	11 - Group 10B	17
24 - 25 - Mexican Serenade	17	16-17 - Choucoune	16	12	18
26 - The I and V7 Chords in G Major	18	18-19 - Freight Train	17	13 - Group 12A	19
27 - Plaisir d'Amour	19	20-21 - A Sentimental Song	18	13 - Group 12B	20
28 - The Primary Chords in G Major	20		19	14	21-22
29 - Why Am I Blue?	21	22-23 - A Syncopated Song	20	15 - Group 14A	23
30 - 31 - Red River Valley	21	24-25 - Under the Stars!	21	15 - Group 14B	24
32 - The D Major Scale	22		22	16	25
33 - Calypso Carnival	22	26 - Pizzicato in D	23	17	26
34 - The I and V7 Chords in D Major	23		24	18 - Group 16A	27
35 - Rock-a My Soul	24	27 - Divertimento in D	25	18 - Group 16B	28
36 - The Primary Chords in D Major	25		26	19	29-30
37 - Walkin' the Basses	26		27	20 - Group 18A	31
38 - 39 - The Syncopated Music Box	27		28	20 - Group 18B	32
40 - 41 - O Sole Mio!		28-29 - Tango in D	29	21 - Group 19A	33
42 - 43 - Stroll in the Park	28-29	30-31 - Sarasponda	30	21 - Group 19B	34
44 - 45 - The Entertainer	30-31		31	22 - After p. 36*	35
46 - Movin' Along	32	32 - Oh! Susanna!	32	23 - After p. 36*	36
47 - Review of Musical Terms					37-38

* use anytime after
page 36

Alfred's Basic Piano Library • Level 1A

Correlation Chart for Lesson Book 1A With this page(s)	Theory 1A Use this page(s)	Recital 1A Use after page(s)	Notespeller 1A Use this page(s)	Technic 1A Use with page(s)	Ear Training 1A Use with page(s)
3 - How to Sit at the Piano					
4 - Fingers Have Numbers					
5 - Piano Tones					
6 - The Keyboard					
7 - Low Sounds and High Sounds					3
8 - Right & Left					
9 - Left & Right					4
10 - Merrily We Roll Along					
11 - O'er the Deep Blue Sea	2-3-4 (use before p.12)				5
12 - Hand-Bells Part 1 (for left hand)	5-6				
13 - Hand-Bells Part 2 (for right hand)	5-6	2 - Echo Song			6
14 - Jolly Old Saint Nicholas, Part 1					
15 - Jolly Old Saint Nicholas, Part 2		3 - Sailor Jack			7
16 -17 - Old MacDonald		3 - Sailor Jack			8
18 - A B C D E F G	7-10				
19 - An Easy Way to Find Any White Key	7-10		3		9
20 - Batter Up!*		4 - Strange Story			
21 - My Clever Pup	11	5 - The Joke's on Us!			10
22 - The Zoo	12	6 - Lost My Partner! & 7 - Old Joe Clark	4-5		
23 - Playing in a New Position	13	8 - Morning Prayer	6	2 - 3	11
24 - Sailing	14				12
25 - Skating	15	9 - Sunshine!	7		13
26 - Wishing Well	15	10 - My Favorite Day!			14
27 - The Staff*	16		8		
28 - The Bass Clef Sign	17		9		
29 - Rain, Rain!	17	11 - Mrs. Murphy's House	10		15
30 - The Treble Clef Sign	18		11		
31 - A Happy Song	18	12 - Gee, We're Glad!	12		16
32 - The Grand Staff*	19		13		
33 - "Position C"	20		14	4 - 5	17
34 - A Happy Song (for both hands)	20	13 - Christopher Columbus	15		18
35 - See-Saws	21				19
36 - Just a Second!	22		16	6 - 7	20
37 - Balloons	23	14 - Come Fly!			21
38 - Who's on Third?*	24	15 - Robin Hood	17		
39 - Mexican Hat Dance	24	15 - Robin Hood			22
40 - More About Intervals	25		18		23
41 - Rock Song	26			8 - 9	24
42 - Rockets	26	16 - Quiet River	19		
43 - Sea Divers	26	16 - Quiet River			25
44 - Play a Fourth	27		20	10 -11	
45 - July the Fourth!*	27	17 - Come to My House!			26
46 - Old Uncle Bill	27		21		27
47 - Love Somebody	28	18 - The Call of the Horn			28
48 - My Fifth	29	19 - Rock Anywhere!	22	12 - 13	
49 - The Donkey	29	20-21 - Favorite Words			29
50 - "Position G"	30		23		
51 - Jingle Bells!	31	22 - Hymn of Praise	24	14 - 15	30
52 - 53 - Willie & Tillie	32	23 - Come Buy My Balloons!	25		
54 - A Friend Like You	33	24-25 - Who Built the Ark?	26		31
55 - My Robot	34		27		32
56 - Rockin' Tune	35	26 - A Riddle (Tumbalalaika)	28	16 -17	
57 - Indian Song	36	26 - A Riddle (Tumbalalaika)	29		33
58 - Raindrops	37	27 - The Popcorn Man	30		34
59 - It's Halloween!*	38-39	28-29 - Charlie, the Chimp!		18 - 19	35
60 - 61 - Horse Sense	40	30 - My Secret Place & 32 - Pastorale	31		36
62 - 63 - Review			32	20 - 21	37

* In the Universal edition of Lesson Book 1A, some of the above titles have been changed: page 20 - Come and Play, page 27 - The Stave, page 32 - The Grand Stave, page 38 - Play a Third, page 45 - Fourths Are Fun!, page 59 - Hide and Seek.

Alfred's Basic Piano Library • Level 1B

Lesson 1B With this page(s)	Theory 1B Use this page(s)	Recital 1B Use after page(s)	Notespeller 1B Use this page(s)	Technic 1B Use with page(s)	Ear Training 1B Use with page(s)
2 - Review	2-3		3		
3 - Step Right Up!	4		4		3
4 - The Carousel	5		5		4
5 - Hail to Thee, America! / Brother John*	6-7			2 - 3	5
6 - Good Sounds	8	2-3 - I've Been Wishin'	6		6
7 - The Cuckoo		4-5 - Hayride!			7
8 - Money Can't Buy Ev'rything!	9	6-7 - Fanfare and Canon	7	4 - 5	8
9 - Ping-Pong	10		8		9
10 - Grandpa's Clock		8-9 - Minuet and Trio			10
11 - When the Saints Go Marching In		8-9 - Minuet and Trio	9		11
12 - G's in the "Bag"	11		10		12
13 - Join the Fun	11	10 - Limerick Tune	11	6 - 7	13
14 - Oom-Pa-pa!	11		12		14
15 - The Clown	12	11 - Hiawatha	13		15
16 - Thumbs on C!	13		14		16
17 - Waltz Time	14	12 - 13 - Anyone for Tic-Tac-Toe?	15	8 - 9	17
18 - Good King Wenceslas	14	14 - Camptown Races			18
19 - The Rainbow	15	15 - For He's a Jolly Good Fellow!	16		19
20 - Good Morning to You!					20
21 - Happy Birthday to You!	16		17	10 - 11	21
22 - Yankee Doodle	17	16 - The Old Mill			22
23 - The Windmill	18	17 - The Gift to Be Simple	18		23
24 - Indians	18	18-19 - The Elephant and the Flea	19		24
25 - New Position G	19		20	12 - 13	25
26 - Pedal Play	20				26
27 - Harp Song	20		21		
28 - Concert Time	20	20-21 - Soaring			27
29 - Music Box Rock	20		22		
30 - 31 - A Cowboy's Song	20		23		28
32 - 33 - The Magic Man	21	22-23 - Freight Train	24	14 - 15	29
34 - 35 - The Greatest Show on Earth!	22-23	24-25 - A Hiding Game	25	16	30
36 - Measuring Half Steps	24		26		
37 - The Whirlwind	24	26-27 - The Storm	26	17 - Group 8C	31
38 - Measuring Whole Steps	25		27		
39 - The Planets	26	28-29 - March of the Extra-Terrestrials	27	17 - Group 8D	32
40 - Tetrachords	27				33
41 - The Major Scale	28		28		34
42 - Carol in G Major	29		29	18 - 19	35
43 - French Lullaby	30	30-31 - Rondino		20	36
44 - 45 - Sonatina	31		30	21	37
46 - When Our Band Goes Marching By!	32	32 - The Caravan	31-32		38
47 - Review of Musical Terms					

* In the Universal edition of Lesson Book 1B, one of the above titles has been changed: page 5 - Let's Go To America!/Brother John.

Alfred's Basic Piano Library • Level 2

Lesson 2 With this page(s)	Theory 2 Use this page(s)	Recital 2 Use after page(s)	Notespeller 2 Use this page(s)	Technic 2 Use with page(s)	Ear Training 2 Use with page(s)
2 - 3 - Get Away!	3	2-3 - Fiesta!	3		3
4 - 5 - Introducing Dotted Quarter Notes	4-5		4		4
6 - Alouette		4-5 - Toymaker's Dance	5	2 - 3	5
7 - Ode to Joy	6	4-5 - Toymaker's Dance	5		6
8 - Measuring 6ths	7		6	4 - Group 2A	
9 - Lavender's Blue	7	6-7 - Bell Song	7	4 - Group 2B	7
10 - When You Grow Up	8		8	5 - Group 2C	8
11 - Kum-ba-yah!	8	8-9 - Rockin' on 6!	8	5 - Group 2D	9
12 - Measuring 6ths in G Position	9		9	6 - 7	
13 - 18th Century Dance	9	10-11 - Bourrée and Musette	10		10
14 - London Bridge			11	8	11
15 - Nick Nack Paddy Wack	10	12-13 - Wash-Day Boogie	12	9	12
16 - 17 - Lone Star Waltz	11	14-15 - Come and Dance the Polka!	13	10 - 11	13
18 - Crossing RH 2 over 1 / Crossing LH 2 over 1	12-13		14	12 - 13	14
19 - On the Bridge at Avignon	14		14	12 - 13	15
20 - 21 - Malagueña	15	16-17 - Evening Song	15	12 - 13	16
22 - Measuring 7ths	16		16	14 - 15	17
23 - Our Special Waltz	16	18-19 - Clementine	17		17
24 - More About the C Major Scale	17		18	16 - 17	18
25 - Prelude	17	20-21 - Tango Staccato	18		19
26 - Measuring Octaves (8ths)	18		19	18 - 19	20
27 - The Can-Can	19	20-21 - Tango Staccato	20		
28 - More About the G Major Scale	20		21	20 - 21	21
29 - The Galway Piper	20	22-23 - Arkansas Traveler	21		22
30 - Triads	21		22	22 - 23	23
31 - Square Dance	22	24-25 - Hoe-Down!	23		24
32 - 33 - Cockles and Mussels	23		24		25
34 - The Primary Triads / Chord Progressions	24-25-26	26 - Waltzing Triads	25	24 - Group 12A	26
35 - Blue Scales	25-26		25	24 - Group 12B	27
36 - V^7 Chord/Primary Chords in C Major	27		26	25 - Group 12C	28
37 - Got Lotsa Rhythm	27	27 - The Streets of Laredo	26	25 - Group 12D	29
38 - The Primary Chords in G Major	28		27	26 - Group 13A	30
39 - Why Am I Blue?			27		
40 - 41 - Red River Valley	29	28 - Plaisir d'Amour	28	26 - 27 Group 13B, C&D	31
42 - D Major Scale	30		29	28	32
43 - Calypso Carnival	30		29		33
44 - The Primary Chords in D Major	31		30	29	34
45 - Oh! Susanna!		29 - Divertimento in D	30		35
46 - 47 - Sarasponda	32	30-31 - Rondo	31-32	30 - 31	36

Alfred's Basic Piano Library • Level 3

Lesson 3 With this page(s)	Theory 3 Use this page(s)	Recital 3 Use after page(s)	Notespeller 3 Use this page(s)	Technic 3 Use with page(s)	Ear Training 3 Use with page(s)
2 - 3 - Goodbye, Old Paint	2-3	2-3 - A Country Song	3	2 - 3	3-4
4 - 5 - On Top of Old Smoky	4	4-5 - The Marines' Hymn	4	4 - Group 2A & B	5
6 - 7 - Festive March	5	6-7 - Down in the Valley	5	5 - Group 2C & D	6
8 - 9 - Alpine Melody	6-7	8-9 - Alpine Polka	6	6 - 7	7-8
10 - 11 - Waltz Pantomime	8-9	10-11 - The Gypsy Baron	7	8 - 9	9
12 - 13 - Light and Blue	10	10-11 - The Gypsy Baron	8		10
14 - 15 - Roman Holiday	11	12-13 - Chiapanecas	9	10 - 11	11
16 - 17 - Prelude	12	12-13 - Chiapanecas	10	12 - 13	12
18 - The Chromatic Scale	13		11	14 - 15	13
19 - Village Dance	13	14-15 - Circus March	12		14
20 - The F Major Scale	14		13	16 - Group 8A & B	15
21 - Casey Jones	15	16-17 - Little Brown Jug	14	17 - Group 8C & D	16
22 - 23 - A Day in Vienna	16-17	18-19 - Teapot Gavotte	15	18 - 19	17-18
24 - Minor Scales	18-19		16	20 - 21	19
25 - Enchanted City	19	20 - Jericho	17		20
26 - More about 3rds / More about 5ths	20-21		18	22 - Group 11A & B	21
27 - Make Up Your Mind!	20-21	21 - Puppet Dance	19		22
28 - 29 - The Major and the Minor	22		20	23 - Group 11C & D	23-24
30 - 31 - Greensleeves	23	22-23 - Spanish Dance	21	24 - 25 Group 12A, B&C	25
32 - 33 - Fandango	24	22-23 - Spanish Dance	22	25 - Group 12D	26
34 - The Primary Triads in Minor Keys	25		23	26 - Group 13A & B	27
35 - Go Down, Moses	25		24		28
36 - 37 - Intermezzo	26	24-25 - Overture	25	27 - Group 13C & D	29
38 - The Key of D Minor (Relative of F Major)	27		26	28 - 29 Group 14A, B&C	30
39 - Scarborough Fair	27		27		31
40 - 41 - Raisins and Almonds	28	26-27 - Introduction and Dance	28	29 - Group 14D	32-33
42 - 43 - Hunting Song	29	28-29 - Furiant	29	30 - Group 15A	34
44 - 45 - La Raspa	30-31	30-31 - Mexican Hat Dance	30	30 - Group 15B	35
46 - 47 - Scherzo	32	30-31 - Mexican Hat Dance	31	31 - Group 15C & D	36

Dictionary of Musical Terms

Accent (>) .... placed over or under a note that gets special emphasis. Play the note louder.

Accidental .... a sharp or flat not given in the key signature.

Adagio .... slowly.

Allegro .... quickly, happily.

Andante .... moving along (at walking speed).

A tempo .... resume original speed.

Block chords .... notes of a chord are played together.

Broken chords .... notes of a chord are played one at a time.

Chord progression .... changing from one chord to another—as an example, I, IV, I, V7, I.

Chromatic scale .... a scale made up entirely of half steps. It uses every key, black and white.

Crescendo (——) .... gradually louder.

Da Capo al Fine (D.C. al Fine) .... repeat from the beginning and play to the Fine (end).

Diminuendo (——) .... gradually slower.

Dynamic signs .... signs showing how loud or soft to play.

Fermata (⌢) .... indicates that a note should be held longer than its true value.

Fine .... the end.

First ending (⌐1.   ⌐) .... the measures under the bracket are played the first time only.

Flat sign (♭) .... lowers a note one half step. Play the next key to the left.

Fortissimo (𝑓𝑓) .... very loud.

Forte (𝑓) .... loud.

Half step .... the distance from one key to the very next one, with no key between.

Harmonic interval .... the interval between two tones sounded together.

Incomplete measure .... a measure at the beginning of a piece with fewer counts than shown in the time signatures. The missing counts are found in the last measure.

Interval .... the difference in pitch (highness or lowness) between two tones.

Key signature .... the number of sharps or flats in any key—written at the beginning of each line.

Legato .... smoothly connected. Usually indicated by a slur over or under the notes.

Major scale .... a series of 8 notes made of two tetrachords joined by a whole step.